———— ROBIN ELLIOTT

CHANGE

A PRACTICAL GUIDE FOR DEALING WITH AND
MANAGING PERSONAL AND PROFESSIONAL CHANGE

**DIGESTIBLE
BUSINESS
LEARNING**

———— QUICKBITES.CO

Copyright © 2017 Robin Elliott

All rights reserved. This book or any portion thereof may not be reproduced or used in any manner whatsoever without the express written permission of the publisher except for the use of brief quotations in a book review or scholarly journal.

First Printing: 2016

Second Printing: 2017

QuickBites

32/101 Miller St

North Sydney NSW 2060

www.quickbites.co

QUICKBITES
DIGESTIBLE BUSINESS LEARNING

TABLE OF CONTENTS

ABOUT ROBIN ELLIOTT i
PREFACE ii
COMPETENCY MAP iii
INTRODUCTION 1

PART 1 : CHANGE AND YOU 3
    REGAINING CONTROL 4

PART 2 : THE REALITY OF CHANGE 19
    NAVIGATING THE FLOW 20
    THE ROLLERCOASTER OF CHANGE 26
    CHANGE: NOISY AND QUIET 28
    THE PERFECTION MYTH 30

PART 3 : CHANGING FOR SUCCESS 34
    THE A4 CHANGE PROCESS 35
    MAKING IT HAPPEN 38
    PERSONAL COMMITMENTS 43
    WRAP UP 44

OTHER QUICKBITE TITLES 45
WANT MORE INFORMATION? 47

ABOUT ROBIN ELLIOTT

Business and Leadership expert Robin Elliott is extensively qualified in people and operational management, having held C-Suite and Asia Pacific roles for a number of multinational and publicly listed corporations. Robin combines her rich corporate experience with a background in academic and executive education to bring you targeted and applicable developmental content.

Robin is qualified with a Bachelor of Business (Curtin University) and a Master of Management (University of Western Australia).

For a full profile on Robin see https://quickbites.co/author

PREFACE

QUICKBITES
Digestible Business Learning

Welcome to QuickBites

QuickBites provides 'bite-sized', digestible content for personal and professional development. Digestible learning integrates concept with practice. It is information that can be applied to everyday situations. It is learning that sticks.

The content in this workbook will help you to close the gap between current problems and desired outcomes by facilitating tangible skills development to ensure personal and professional efficiency, effectiveness and productivity. The learning process will strengthen the key competencies required for commercial success.

QuickBites books can be used either as individual guides to help you build your skills, ready-made workbook content for workshops and training sessions or supplementary material to focus and enhance your coaching activities.

At the heart of all QuickBites resources is the belief that active self-enquiry and individual accountability is the way to build awareness and growth. The reflective and self-assessment exercises within QuickBites are an important tool to engage you fully in the developmental journey.

To help you synthesise the content and highlight the key practical points, QuickBites presents you with a unique insights summary at the end of each section. This feature helps you to quickly arrive at the main applications and understandings and accelerates your learning and skill development.

The practical application of useful theory, universal examples, exercises, templates and self-assessment activities will develop and strengthen the essential abilities required for personal and business achievement.

Use QuickBites, and fast track your way to success.

COMPETENCY MAP

The content of this book and its learning objectives address the following competencies:

CLUSTER	COMPETENCY
CREATING THE NEW AND DIFFERENT	• Dealing with Ambiguity • Perspective • Strategic Agility
DEMONSTRATING PERSONAL FLEXIBILITY	• Personal learning • Self Development • Self-Knowledge
MANAGING UP	• Career Ambition
BALANCING WORK/LIFE	• Work/Life Balance

Based on Laminger Competencies

INTRODUCTION

"It's not that we fear change, it's that we fear losing control"

Change is the constant companion in both our personal and professional life. Change affects us at an individual level, as we negotiate the reality of our personal growth and development, and as managers and leaders in the organisation when we impose change upon others.

Wisdom informs us of the nature of impermanence, that all things come to pass. Given change is such a constant dynamic, coping with change should be second nature. Yet as we know, change is the very thing that we resist and fear and find most difficult. Change goes to the heart of our vulnerability, as invariably we feel that we are not in control. Learning to understand our own personal change process, as well as how it presents in others, is a crucial skill for personal and professional effectiveness.

What we fear most is not change itself, but the unknown, and the subsequent loss of control. Understanding change is the first step in helping us negotiate this unfamiliar. Being able to identify the common emotional reactions and the typical manifestations of change, as well as having practical and tangible strategies to deal with change in ourselves and others, assists us to not only survive change, but thrive within it.

REFLECTION

1. Are you good or bad at dealing with change?
   _____
   _____

2. Given your answer to question 1, why do you think this is so?
   _____
   _____

3. What are your biggest challenges when dealing with change?
   _____
   _____

4. Can you identify a usual pattern that you have in relation to dealing with change?
   _____
   _____

5. Think of a time when you coped with significant change. What were you experiencing at the time? What emotions were you feeling? What helped you to move through the change process?
   _____
   _____

PART 1

CHANGE AND YOU

REGAINING CONTROL

Creating Your North Star

*"Change mastery occurs when we live life deliberately,
when we are at the cause of change rather than the effect"*

The key reason change causes unrest and ill-ease is that we feel we are not in control. Change alters our reality. Change removes those external reference points we have used to form our lives, such as our job or our relationship, and in doing so increases anxiety about where we are we going and what's next.

One way to lessen the concerns that change causes when our external reality is shifting is to have us return to an inner reference point, our own north star. The north star is that fixed star in the sky that aligns with true north. For centuries it was used by explorers to set a direction. When historical explorers didn't know where they were heading, they would refer to the north star as a continued source of certainty.

Change is easier when we're prepared for it and when we feel we have had some hand in its occurrence. Change mastery occurs when we live life deliberately, when we are at the cause of change rather than the effect. We deal better with change when we can be proactive and think about what we want from life, rather than being reactive and have life happen to us.

Creating our own metaphorical north star assists us to be proactive. A personal north star serves to create an inner compass. It helps us to anchor to an internal locus of control and is a steady reference point against which to make decisions. A personal north star becomes a barometer for us so that we can gauge our actions with two simple questions:

"Does this decision align with my north star?";

and

"Does it take me closer or further away?"

What's a Personal North Star?

*"Having your own north star enables **you** to become the anchor in the storm"*

Our personal north star takes its form in 3 areas:

1. What we decide are our values;

2. What we have as our vision;

3. What we think is our purpose.

These 3 life foundations are our inner drivers, those feelings and urges that drive us to choose one course of action over another.

Having a north star enables you to become the anchor in the storm. A north star allows you to live life from the inside out, because you operate from a solid and stable inner point of security. This empowers you to choose how you want to impact your environment. There is always a choice, a decision to be made, which can simply be the attitude you adopt in response to a situation. Ask yourself; *"Do I get down and dirty, mirror the chaos and amplify the problem, or do I rise up and stand bright? Do I instead become the calm centre, the antidote, the opposing counterweight to the imbalance?"*

Think about which of these attitudes you usually adopt.

It is important to have a process to decide on these 3 important north star components. This process builds awareness and understanding, the two vital components to enabling conscious and deliberate choices and mastery over change.

Let's explore this process now, by firstly looking at some examples of north stars, and then working through the 3 step process.

North Stars in Action

Sally had a long and successful career behind her, but her life had shifted. She now had 2 teenage children, and she felt she needed to spend more time with them. Her north star became work/life balance, and she passed up a major promotion because it would have meant more time away from home. Instead of feeling like she'd failed, she realised she was simply following her own inner desires and wishes. And she was happy.

John had a major dream to be self-employed. He took a series of contract roles, rather than a full-time job, as a way of supporting himself whilst he built his business. When jobs came to him, he negotiated for them to be done on a contract basis.

Chris had a dream to work internationally. He joined a global company where he made his career aspirations known. He worked hard and stayed with the company even when he had another job offer. After 3 years, with a solid internal reputation, he was transferred overseas.

Step 1. Deciding on Your Values

Values are those things we hold to be true. They are our beliefs about the world, our 'non-negotiables.' Deciding on what we believe is true and what we cannot compromise on is a key step to creating an inner point of reference.

What we believe about the world and ourselves determines our behaviour and our decisions. For example, if we have a value of cooperation and think that is a more true value than competition, we are more likely to share knowledge and advice with our colleagues and not compete with them by withholding information. If we value freedom above all else, we may decide to be self-employed, or we may choose to stay single rather than commit to a relationship. Our inner drivers will shape our outer reality. They are the cause to our effect.

A useful analogy to understanding how values shape our outer reality is comparing the process to the structure of an iceberg.

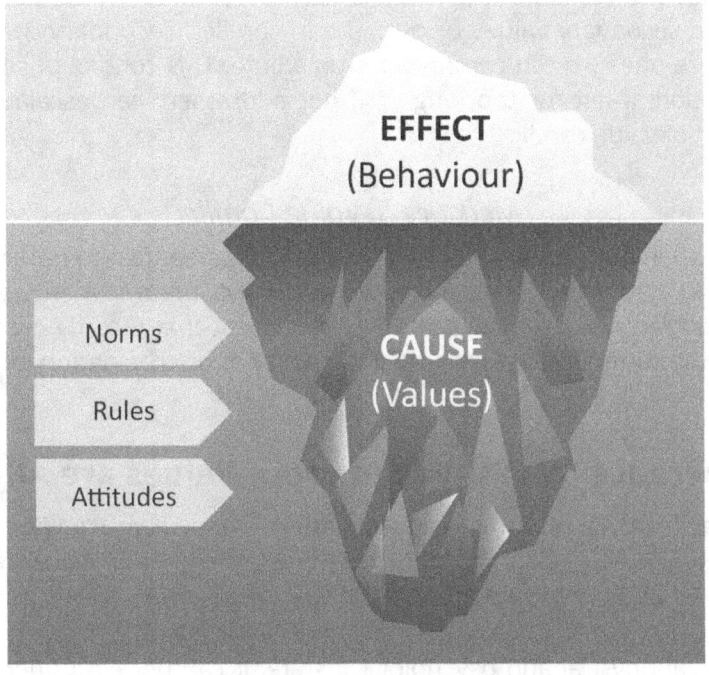

Figure 1: The Iceberg Effect

As the diagram in Figure 1 shows, values are the cause to the effect. Above the water line, 'visible' behaviour, is dictated by our beliefs and what we hold to be true. Values shape our attitudes, our norms and ultimately our own internal rules, what we believe we can and can't do. Attempting to change our behaviour without examining the internal beliefs that have driven that outward expression will only ever result in superficial change.

How to Measure Values: Alignment, Conflict and Agitation

Value assessment is a useful process to have us understand the source of our contentment and dissatisfaction. There are 3 types of value measures we can use to assess how our individual values affect us. These measures help us to evaluate our decision making and our environments, and how these factors are playing into our happiness or discontent.

Measure 1. Value Alignment

Value alignment is when the situation we find ourselves in, and the decisions and choices we make, are in line with our most important values and those beliefs we hold sacrosanct, such as honesty. For example, we have value alignment when we work in an organisation that values the same things that we do, that behaves as we would, that makes the decisions from a guidance system that is the same as our own. Value alignment is what we strive for because it is a state of, by and large, contentment.

Measure 2. Value Agitation

Value agitation is a subtle state of discontent and is the most common value state we experience. Value agitation occurs when secondary values of ours are in conflict. Secondary values are those that are important to us but are ones we can compromise on a little. This conflict of secondary values causes agitation. Value agitation, if left for too long or if not addressed, can escalate into a deeper, more entrenched state, that of value conflict.

Measure 3. Value Conflict

Value conflict occurs when our primary values, those that are steadfast to us, are in direct conflict with the situation we are in or the choice we make. Value conflict occurs when we are making decisions against our most important values, or are in an environment that directly conflicts with our primary values. For example, the company may have a subtle policy of discrimination, or may even be engaged in some illegal activity.

Coherence: When We Know our Values are Aligned

Psychologists at HeartMath (a research and education organisation) advise that to keep calm in stressful circumstances you must shift to a state known as coherence. Coherence is a state of unity and integration, in which the body and mind are together and at ease.

Coherence is a very real physical and psychological state. It can be felt. Coherence comes when our values are aligned, and when we are on track with our north star.

Getting to coherence is a many-faceted journey, but it starts from going within, assessing what's important, and then from that inner place, examining your environment for sources of value agitation and conflict. This is the inside-out approach that helps us on the path to change mastery. This approach means we adopt a more proactive stance, and move more deliberately through life. It allows us to make targeted and focused changes, which are likely to be more permanent and effective.

PART 1 : CHANGE AND YOU

ACTIVITY: VALUE ASSESSMENT

(See the Values Assessment Card Sort, a companion Quick Bites product, at (https://quickbites.co)

1. Consider the following suggested values. Using the table below, sort the values into most important, important, and least important. Add your own values if they are not in this picture.

respect honesty courage tact friendliness clarity innovative moderation trust humility loyalty discipline commitment team flexibility collaboration responsibility justice understanding diligence assertiveness modesty confidence unity creativity tolerance speed patience excellence

MOST IMPORTANT	IMPORTANT	LEAST IMPORTANT

CHANGE - A Practical Guide

2. Given the values you have chosen, reflect on past actions and behaviours. How do you think your most important values have shaped your choices and decision making?

   _____

   _____

3. Now consider a current life situation, whether that be a work or personal situation, that is causing you discontent. Describe it here:

   _____

   _____

4. Using the table below, assess this situation against your values, by deciding what components of it are either aligned, somewhat aligned, or not aligned. For example if you are in a job where your value of collaboration is repeatedly being violated by the actions of your boss, then you would place collaboration against the 'not aligned' category.

ALIGNED	SOMEWHAT ALIGNED	NOT ALIGNED

5. Name a time you have experienced coherence, whether that be in a particular situation or a period of your life. What was happening? What were the essential qualities of this situation/period? What does this tell you about how to create coherence for yourself now and in the future?

   _____

   _____

PART 1 : CHANGE AND YOU

REFLECTION

1. What is your immediate reaction to the answers you have provided in the value assessment?

   _____
   _____
   _____

2. What do your answers tell you about the current situation and/or decision you are dealing with?

   _____
   _____
   _____

3. What could be some steps you could take to resolve the situation?

   _____
   _____
   _____

Step 2: Creating Your Personal Vision

"Deciding what we'd like from our future makes it more likely that we'll get there"

The second step in the process of deciding on our north star is having a personal vision. Deciding what we'd like from our future makes it more likely we'll get there. The following activities are designed to help you form your vision and give you the time and focus to assess and identify what you want.

In order to make changes to our life, we have to start from where we are right now. We can't create a better future without first examining our current situation, and deciding what's working and what's not.

Taking a personal inventory helps us to decide what we want more of in our life, and what we want less of.

Let's explore this now.

PART 1 : CHANGE AND YOU

ACTIVITY
Vision Stage 1: Present Day Stocktake

Take some time to think about the main areas of your life and the attention and focus you are giving them. Using the categories below – draw a blank pie chart and allocate the sections as you are currently experiencing them in your life. For example you may be focusing 50% of your time per week on work, 10% of your time on 'me' time, 10% on your relationship and so on. If these categories don't work exactly for you alter to fit.

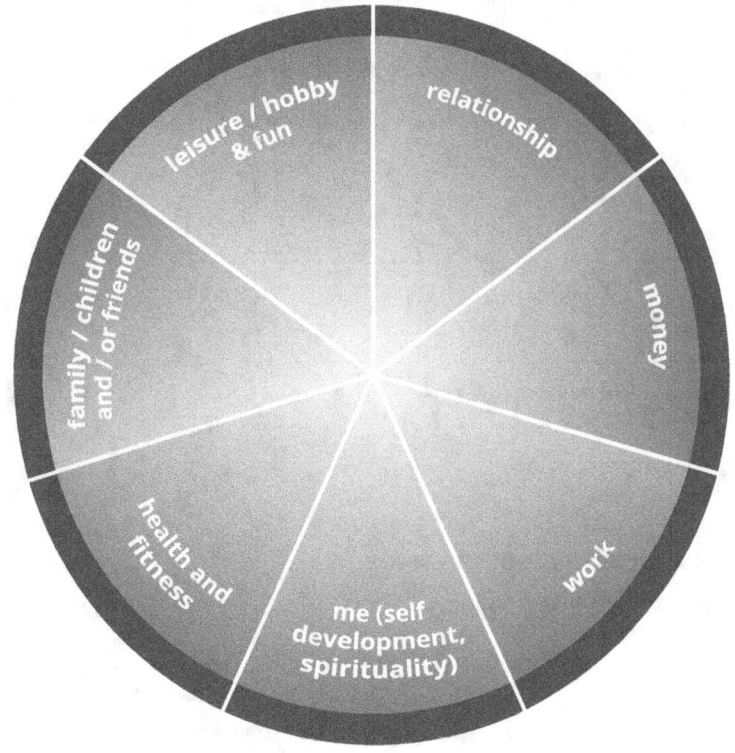

CHANGE - A Practical Guide

REFLECTION

1. What is your immediate reaction to the pie chart you have drawn?

_____

_____

2. How does it look? In each of the areas think about what it is that you are enjoying and not enjoying.

_____

_____

3. What would you like less of and more of from your life and career?

_____

_____

HOW SHOULD IT LOOK?

Given your answers above, now draw the pie chart as you would like it to look.

PART 1 : CHANGE AND YOU

Vision Stage 2: Your Letter From the Future

"Imagination points to all we might yet discover and create" – Albert Einstein

After we've completed our present day stocktake, the next step is to project our self to the future. We do this by writing a letter to our self from the future. Writing from a future tense is a fun way to help us form our personal vision.

Choose a date in the future at least 12 months from now. Imagine that you have travelled in time to this future date and you are sitting down writing a letter back to your present day self.

Write about how great your life and work is now, what you are enjoying most, what you have achieved and how you've reduced the things that you didn't want in your life. Try to imagine and feel how this future life is. Write about your emotions and use those words that adequately describe how you might be feeling. Be creative and don't censor yourself.

TIP: When you construct this letter, focus on writing from a state of coherence. Write about the positive things that you would like to have happening and how you are feeling. Include your values in your letter and write about how these are operating in your new life.

Take 30-40 minutes and write your Letter from the Future

LETTER FROM THE FUTURE

Dear

Vision Step 3 Closing The Gap

Now you have 3 foundations to work with:

- you know your values and have prioritised them, you know what your 'non-negotiables' are;

- you have conducted a personal present day stocktake, which has allowed you to understand what you want more of and what you want less of;

- you have projected yourself to your future, and can feel it and imagine it as already being here.

Now, you are ready to create your personal north star.

Examples of Personal North Stars

Personal north stars are best written as 'I am' statements, and incorporate your most important values and your vision and related goals for the future.

"I am a creative leader who does not compromise on honesty and personal freedom. I am here to assert my independence and purpose through operating my own successful business."

"I am a vital cog in the wheel who champions respect, discipline and courage. I will fulfil my purpose by obtaining a senior operational role within the business."

"I am passionate about friendship and authenticity. I strive to make every interaction I have with others meaningful and beneficial. This will help me to increase my networks and build my coaching practice."

"I have a healthy work/life balance and strong boundaries. I make time for my family and my work serves their growth and fulfilment."

PART 1 : CHANGE AND YOU

What's Your North Star?

MY NORTH STAR

I am

QUICKBITES INSIGHTS

We resist change because we fear losing control.

Your personal North Star is your internal anchor point and helps you to be at the cause of change rather than at the effect.

Creating your north star starts with a clear intent which results in a future vision.

There are 3 foundations to creating your personal vision.

Foundation 1: Know your values.

Foundation 2: Conduct a present day personal stock take.

Foundation 3: Project yourself to your future and feel it as if it has already happened.

Personal North Stars are written as 'I am' statements.

North stars incorporate your most important values, your vision and related future goals.

PART 2

THE REALITY OF CHANGE

NAVIGATING THE FLOW

"Consider all change to be good, otherwise it wouldn't be happening"

The way to cope with change starts with adopting the right mindset. Accepting that change is a constant in life is a good place to start.

Change invariably brings disorder and is disruptive. It can even be downright scary. But we have a choice to view this disorder in another way. We can view it as clearing the way to become 'suitable for something else.'

Becoming Suitable for Something Else

Change creates shifts, both psychological and physiological.

These shifts invariably create a process where the old leaves in order to make way for the new. This can mean a breaking of habits and mental patterns, and it can also mean tangible physical changes such as a new job, a new home or a new relationship.

When the new is taking shape, both within us and outside of ourselves, we feel vulnerable. This vulnerability is at the heart of why we resist change, because vulnerability takes down our defences and, for a time, puts us in a place of minimal control. Vulnerability represents the juncture of our future coming in to shake hands with our present. It represents a watershed of events and emotion which is anything but comfortable, but which ultimately is there to ensure the future not only takes hold, but succeeds.

And yet, if we trust in the wisdom of our own life process, we can settle into change and strap ourselves in for the ride. If we adjust our mindsets, we see that change results in the old forms of our life not fitting, like a size of clothing that is too small or too big. The structure of our internal and external life must change to accommodate the bigger, more expansive, truer and more powerful version of ourselves.

Understanding how we typically react to change, and gaining awareness of our mindset, helps us to better navigate the flow of change as we optimise the most beneficial approach.

How Do I React To Change?

You have faced changes or new situations in your life many times before. Look at the pairs of words or statements on the following page and select which words best describe the way you go about facing changes or new situations in your work or personal life.

If you identify strongly with the word on the left, tick A. Tick B if less strongly. If you identify with the word on the right tick C and tick D if you identify strongly with the word on the right.

PART 2 : THE REALITY OF CHANGE

1234 TABLE

	1	2	3	4	
Intuitive					Logical
Personally Involved					Personally Objective
Emotional					Intellectual
Supportive					Critical
Eager to discuss with others					Prone to Analysis
Interested in new experiences					Interested in new ideas
A believer in opinion					A believer in theory
Accepting					Questioning
Feeling					Thinking
A quick risk taker					A slow risk taker
Tend to trial and error					Tend to plan and organize
People orientated					Task orientated
Ready to jump in					Wanting facts first
Look for support from others					Look to do it by myself
Total Each Column					

CHANGE - A Practical Guide

Now do the same for the following pairs of words marked 1 to 4 (i.e. I tend to be:):

ABCD TABLE

	A	B	C	D	
Talking					Listening
Acting					Reacting
Taking Small Steps					Looking at the Big Picture
Being Quick					Being Deliberative
Experimenting					Digesting
Looking to Change					Thinking Up ideas
Being Animated					Being Reserved
Doing					Watching
Pursuing Goals					Pursuing Methods for Achievement
Being Practical					Seeking "ideals"
Changing as I Go					Planning in Advance
Finding Solutions					Identifying problems
Thinking Up Answers					Thinking Up Questions
Total Each Column					

What's Your Style?

Take your highest score from the ABCD table. Was it for column A B C or D? On the table below, draw a dotted line from the top to bottom of the table starting at the letter that was your highest score.

Take your highest score from the 1234 table. Was it for column 1 2 3 or 4? Now draw a straight line across the table below, starting at the number that was your highest score.

Mark where the dotted lines intersect. This is the quadrant that represents your usual coping style when faced with change or a new situation.

NB. You may have more than one coping style. If your intersecting lines fall in the outside corners it will be a style that you hold to very strongly.

	A	B	C	D	
		FEELING			
1.					
		Enthusiastic		Imaginative	
2.					
DOING					**OBSERVING**
3.					
		Practical		Logical	
4.					
		THINKING			

Examining the Styles

Each change style has its own strengths and weaknesses. Examine the following table to assess your own abilities when dealing with change.

CHANGE - A Practical Guide

LOGICAL COPING STYLE

RISK AVERSE/CAUTIOUS

A good theory builder

Puts ideas together to form a new model

Precise and thorough

Redesigns, re-tests, digests

Calculates probabilities

Reacts slowly and wants facts

Works independently, thinking, reading

Avoids over involvement

Pushes mind, analyses ideas

Rational and logical, complete

Learns individually thinking through ideas and designing a plan or model in an organised, sequential way.

IMAGINATIVE COPING STYLE

RISK EMBRACE

Sees lots of alternatives – the whole picture

Uses imagination

Creates with intuition, insight, aesthetic interest

Dislikes routine

Adapts to situations well

Willing to try, jump in

Can be impulsive

Good at seeing, imagining self in different situations

Unhurried, casual, calm, avoids conflict, friendly

Uses eyes, ears, listens, observes, asks questions

Timing important, can't push details until ready

Learns by listening, perceiving, then sharing ideas with others

Likes risks, excitement, change and incentives

PRACTICAL COPING STYLE

RISK RESISTANT

Applies ideas to solving problems

Is cautious

Makes theories useful

Has detective skills, searches and solves

Test hypotheses objectively

Organised, follows a plan

Uses reason and logic

Speculates on alternatives

Likes to be in control

Sets up projects, pilots with research

Acts independently, then gets feedback

Uses factual data, books and theories

Responsible, takes action

Learns by working at probabilities and testing them out.

ENTHUSIASTIC COPING STYLE

RISK READY

Gets involved with lots of new activities

Operates on trial and error and gut reaction

Gets other opinions, feelings, information depends on them

Creates with emotion, senses

Learns by listening, perceiving, then sharing ideas with others

Involves and inspires other people

Searches, seeks out new experiences

Orientated to relationship with people, supportive

Adapts to situations well

Willing to try, jump in

Can be impulsive

Likes learning with people through projects, discussion, 'doing'

Likes assurance from others

PART 2 : THE REALITY OF CHANGE

REFLECTION

1. Given your change style, what are your top strengths when dealing with change?

   _____

   _____

2. Examine the style that you least relate to and decide what you may be missing out on by not embracing the strengths of this style.

   _____

   _____

3. Given your north star and personal vision, how might this style affect the success of staying true to your north star?

   _____

   _____

4. What can you commit to in order to improve your change coping style and ensure you hold firm to your north star?

   _____

   _____

THE ROLLERCOASTER OF CHANGE

Kubler-Ross Change Curve

The Change Curve is based on a model originally developed in the 1960s by Elisabeth Kubler-Ross, a Swiss-American psychiatrist, to explain the grieving process. Since then it has been widely utilised as a method of helping people understand their reactions to significant change or upheaval.

The original five stages of grief – denial, anger, bargaining, depression and acceptance – have been adapted and interpreted over the years. There are numerous versions of the curve in existence. However, the majority of them are consistent in their use of the following basic emotions to explain change and transition, which are often grouped into three distinct transitional stages.

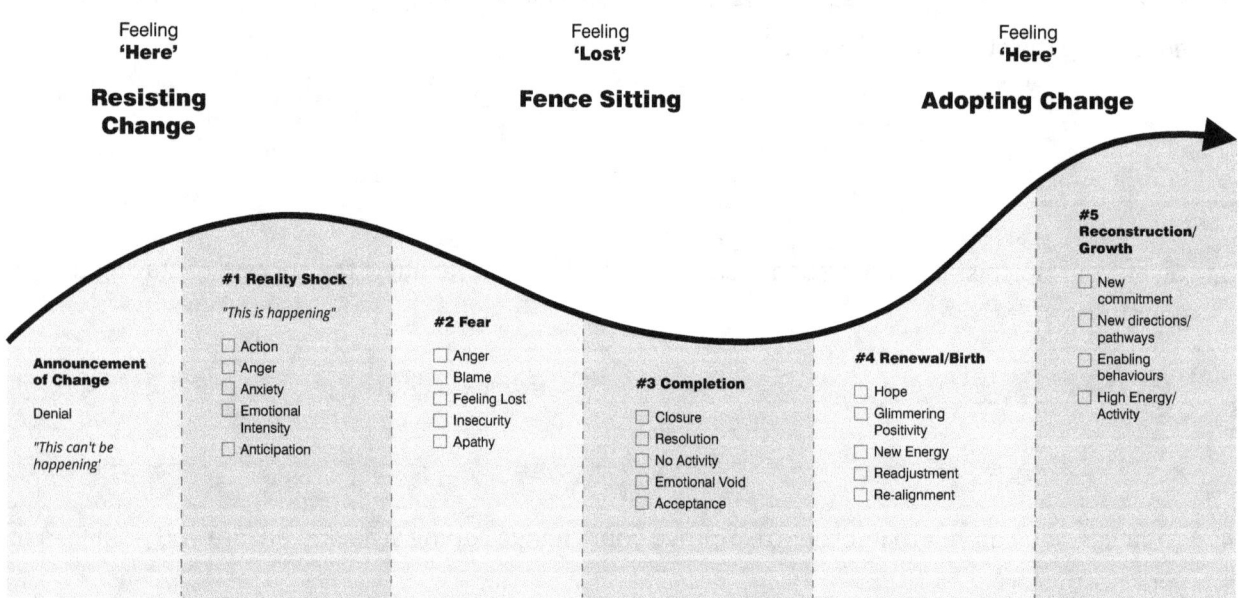

Using The Model

The model shows the transition points of change and the usual emotional state attached to that transition. There are some important points to capture regarding the process, and some useful tips to explain how to move through the process effectively.

Key Points

- Change will always provoke this process.
- Change is a continuum, and you need to move through it.
- What will vary is the time the individual takes to move through each stage.
- You can get stuck in stage 2 and 3, which will prevent you from moving into stage 4 and 5.

- You need to build and practice constructive behaviours in stage 2 and 3 so that you move quickly through these transitions and out the other side.
- The model is not necessarily linear. You may drop back into earlier stages if you haven't completely processed the emotion associated with the particular stage. Typically, this will occur if you are 'triggered' by a similar event, which will cause a state called 'secondary grief'.

The key to applying this model is to understand firstly that change is an emotional process which you must work through. Labelling the stages allows you to better ready yourself for what's coming, and eases the anxiety about anticipating what's next.

Another strategy that the model gives us is to think of ways you can prop up the dip in the curve (stage 2 & 3) so that it is as flat as possible. You do this by practicing constructive behaviours.

What are these behaviours? Let's examine them now.

The Importance of Constructive Behaviours

Constructive behaviours are supportive behaviours. They start with having a firm inner reference point, as we have just explored through the north star exercise. A north star will help you to balance the changes occurring in your external reality against the steady anchor that you have created within.

Remember that our fear of change stems from anxiety about a perceived loss of control. The key to propping up the dip in the curve is to replace control in whatever way you can.

What does this look like? See the following tips and examples:

- Keep to your usual routines as much as possible to reinforce certainty and familiarity. For example, if you've lost your job and you normally walk the dog every morning, or take the children to school or exercise etc., continue to do that.
- Seek professional help. Isolation will lengthen the time you stay in stage 2 & 3. Talk to friends and experts.
- Join a group, whether that is a group aligned to your situation or simply a community group of some description. To repeat, do not isolate yourself.

CHANGE: NOISY AND QUIET

"There is nothing in a caterpillar that tells you it is going to become a butterfly" - Buckminster Fuller

Change is not always external, it is not always about activity and visibility. We often think that to grow, we need to be doing things and making things happen, that we need to be noisy. But if the caterpillar fights to take action when it is cocooned, it will disrupt the natural metamorphous process. If it emerges from the protective covering too early, it will be misshapen and ill-formed. It will, quite simply, be an ineffective and unattractive butterfly.

The stages a caterpillar goes through to become a butterfly is a useful metaphor for your personal change process, in that successful transformation will encompass what can be labelled as both noisy and quiet growth.

Quiet growth is very often about restriction and limitation. It is this development that is often the most difficult to endure as we feel as if nothing is happening, and it heightens the perception that we are not in control.

But inactivity has its place, because it is at this time that psychological change is taking root, and most importantly, it signals an integration of the old and the new. Integration is when coherence occurs; when we break old habits, create new ones, and embody new behaviours.

We will know what type of change we are going through because of our feelings and motivations. When we are experiencing quiet change, we often feel unable to do what we once did; the old behaviours, people, situations seeming oddly out of place. Or, an external event may literally restrict us from doing what we once did. For example, we may be unwell, or our car may have broken down and be in need of repairs. Very often, if we can't stop, something else will come in from our external reality and make us.

When we are going through noisy growth, the opposite will occur. You will be motivated to take action. You may be given extra support, in terms of an additional form of income or a helping hand from a friend or colleague, or you may receive some external feedback which validates your new course of action. In short, you will be inspired to make whatever needs to happen, happen.

We need to respect that change is two-fold, and we also need to recognise that quiet change is often far more demanding than noisy change.

But as the caterpillar knows, quiet growth is ultimately the most rewarding of all.

PART 2 : THE REALITY OF CHANGE

REFLECTION

1. What type of change are you experiencing right now? Quiet or Noisy?

_____
_____

2. Outline your reasons why you think this is so (e.g. you may be experiencing restriction through some external event, or you are motivated to be busy and make physical changes).

_____
_____

3. Are you resisting the current stage of change you are in? Why?

_____
_____

4. What can you do right now to help you manage the change successfully?

_____
_____

THE PERFECTION MYTH

Addressing Your Inner Critic

"You are not perfect, you are a perfect work in progress"

None of us is perfect. What's more, it is a myth that we will ever be perfect. Instead, consider that you are always, a perfect work in progress.

What drives us to seek perfection? We are driven to be faultless because of the existence of the inner critic. The inner critic is that voice inside our head that expresses frustration, criticism or disapproval of our actions. It might sound like, 'why didn't you?" "you shouldn't," "you're hopeless," or "you always mess up."

The voice of the inner critic has its origins in a good place; the place of caution and reason. Our inner critic is the voice that would have us question rather than accept blindly whatever comes our way, the voice that keeps us safe and in control. But over the years, the voice becomes louder, more distorted and over-used, and can dominate us to such an extent that it keeps us stuck and resistant to change.

Engaging the Inner Critic

The trick to dealing with your inner critic is to demystify it so it loses its power. Like any bully, it will back down when confronted.

This next exercise is a powerful and quick way to engage with your inner critic and gain clarity as to its main themes. Very often you will gain insight on the formation of your inner critic and whether that comes from cultural or more personal influences. The key is to time this exercise and do it quickly. You need to act intuitively and not censor yourself.

PART 2 : THE REALITY OF CHANGE

ACTIVITY: A LETTER TO YOUR INNER CRITIC

You are to identify your inner critic as an object, country or animal.

Without thinking too much, what is the first thing that comes to mind? Go with that first thought.

Now set your timer to 10 minutes and write a letter to that object, country or animal.

When the timer goes off, reset it for another 10 minutes, turn around and write a letter back to yourself from your inner critic, as represented by the object, country or animal you have chosen.

Examples

Letters have been written to a doormat, Saudi Arabia, a bull, a crocodile and ballet pointe shoes. Each time, participants have been surprised by the association and the powerful and insightful narrative that surfaces.

Trudy associated her lack of personal boundaries and people pleasing with the obvious analogy of being trodden on like a doormat. Rachael related her lack of empowerment as a woman in business with the restrictions that women experience in Saudi Arabia. Robert realised that the metaphor of a bull typified his constant need to dominate and take charge, while the ballet pointe shoes was an illuminating connection for Penny's exhausting need for perfection.

REFLECTION

1. What is your inner critic trying to do for you?

   _____
   _____

2. How might you now reach a truce with your inner critic and cooperate with it rather than fight against it?

   _____
   _____

3. What is your new affirmation that supports this truce? For example; 'I now own my voice," "I give myself permission to relax," "I assert my own needs."

   _____
   _____

4. How will this new affirmation help you to change?

   _____
   _____

PART 2 : THE REALITY OF CHANGE

QUICKBITES INSIGHTS

To successfully cope with change you need to change your mindset.

Consider that all change is good for you, otherwise it wouldn't be happening.

The change curve teaches us to identify and label the stage we are in, which eases anxiety.

Labelling our change stage allows us to adopt appropriate behaviours and implement actions.

Implement constructive behaviours during the rollercoaster of change so that you can flatten out the curve.

Change is always about you *'becoming suitable for something else.'*

Change can be noisy or quiet. Tune into your feelings and motivations to understand which change you are experiencing.

The way to deal with your inner critic is to engage with it and demystify it.

You do not have to be perfect, you need to be a perfect work in progress.

PART 3

CHANGING FOR SUCCESS

PART 3 : CHANGING FOR SUCCESS

THE A4 CHANGE PROCESS

"Change happens successfully when we are able to align our actions with new knowledge"

4 Steps to Successful Change

Change happens successfully when we are able to align our actions with new knowledge. The process of change is very real, and can be explained through the QuickBites A4 model, a change process that highlights 4 distinct stages, as illustrated below.

Awareness

Personal change starts with an awareness of our current behaviour and actions. There must be a moment when we see clearly, when the veils of denial or illusion fall away and we have a moment of understanding. It can be likened to an epiphany or 'a-ha' moment. Awareness is when we have clarity. Awareness can be imposed upon us through an external event, or it can happen as a process of accumulation, a point in time which has been created by all that has gone before it. Awareness is crucial because we can't change what we don't acknowledge.

Assistance

When that moment of awareness descends, it is important to then seek assistance. The act of awareness creates a space. Awareness represents a metaphorical intervention, it literally creates a break in an existing habit or pattern, and is an opportunity to open up to the new. It is a moment when our resistance to difference is lowered. Seeking assistance is the act of obtaining new knowledge. The form of this new knowledge can be in books, coaching, counselling or by placing yourself deliberately in new environments or situations.

Apply

Knowledge without application will create superficial change only. Knowledge can give us understanding, but if we don't take it that one step further, and connect the knowledge to our everyday lives, it will just sit outside of ourselves, with no discernible effect. We need to *internalise* the new knowledge, accept it and apply it. Application happens because we want it and we allow it. To apply the new, is to say No to the old and to make a decision; a decision that says the status quo cannot remain.

This can be a difficult stage of change, as very often it can take the form of disruption. As we start to connect with and integrate the new knowledge, the new thinking can literally start to reorganise the structure and form of our lives. People or circumstances can leave us and situations can come to 'a head'. In addition, all those people who had invested themselves in our old habits, who were connected to our older self, are likely to resist the change, because if we change, it means they have to change too.

This stage of change is the transformative stage. It is the stage when ice melts to water, when the butterfly starts to emerge from the cocoon. It is the stage where form changes shape, where something new is birthed.

Activate

The activation stage of change builds on the momentum gained from the previous stages, and ensures that the change is embedded in our psyches and our lives. This is the stage where we take the transformation that has occurred *internally*, and translate that into *external* action.

This stage of change is tangible. It is when we take on a new job or leave an old one, when we move to another town, state or country, when we change our intimate relationships.

The activation stage is when we harness our courage and faith, take action, and make the change real.

ACTIVITY: USING THE A4 PROCESS

Think of a current change situation you are dealing with. Drawing on the Rollercoaster of Change and the new knowledge you have gained, use the following table to apply the A4 process.

	The A4 Change Process		
A4 Stage	What's Happening? (Label the Activity or Emotion)	What Am I Resisting? Why Am I Reistsing?	What Can I Do To Help Me Move Through This Stage?
Awareness			
Assistance			
Apply			
Activate			

MAKING IT HAPPEN

Having a Plan

Now that we have taken a journey through the process and reality of change, and better understand the dynamics of change, we are in a better position to master change. Remember that we fear change because we fear the loss of control, so the knowledge presented so far is designed to bring you back to a sense of control and balance.

The final step to regaining control is to have a plan. This plan is one which embodies your north star and enables you to create a pathway towards that north star.

Follow the Breadcrumbs

Sometime the best and only thing you can do is 'follow the breadcrumbs'. Understand that laying down a workable path for change requires 'connectors'. Connectors are people or events that can give you clues as to what to do next, or they can facilitate the next part of the plan through concrete assistance or advice. Be alert and follow your hunches.

Goal Setting

Goals are necessary tools to have us shape our future and live an active and engaged life. Goal setting establishes a target, a point of focus to serve as the reason for our actions. Research shows that people who set goals are more successful in life.

PART 3 : CHANGING FOR SUCCESS

Top Ten Tips for Goal Setting and Planning

1. **Write Down Your Goal.** Writing a goal gives it form and makes it physical. The written word engages the limbic part of your brain which is concerned with action and implementation.

2. **Time Define Your Goal.** Write a start date. Write an end date (30 days, 12 months or 3 years are usual time frames). Write down exactly what you're going to do, record on paper and stick to the plan.

3. **Find Supporters.** We don't change alone. Who will you turn to when you need encouragement? If you don't have a good answer to this, you need to think it through. Make the commitment to your particular supporters and ask them to help you when you hit rough spots. Make a promise to contact them if you do. Put this in your written plan.

4. **Chunk it Down.** A common roadblock to change and goal setting is that we start too big. Ensure you are on the path to success by breaking large goals into smaller, more achievable components.

5. **Create Milestones.** How will you know you're on the right track? Think about particular milestones that will indicate to you that you are making progress.

6. **Log Progress.** Logging progress helps you to reach your goals. Logging progress reminds you to be consistent by maintaining focus and awareness of what you're actually doing. It motivates you towards achievements.

7. **Make Time To Reflect.** Reflect often on your goals, progress and north star. Engaging with the change process and your life is something you should regularly dedicate time to.

8. **Setbacks Happen.** Sometimes we can take 2 steps forward and 3 steps backwards. Setbacks happen. The key is to not just give up after failure, but to reset your resolve. Look at what went wrong and why, understand what you can learn from the situation and pick yourself up and start again.

9. **Revise as Necessary.** The paradox of making a plan is that we have to walk the balance between holding to the plan while knowing when to revise or change it. Make a habit of reflecting on your goals and updating or revising them as necessary.

10. **Keep Active and Connected.** Follow the Breadcrumbs. When appropriate share your goals and plans with others, look for signs and follow your intuition. You never know who can be a bridge to the next step in your plan.

CHANGE - A Practical Guide

MY CHANGE AND TRANSITION PLAN

My North Star
Refer to my north star and record it here:

My Current Mindset
How might my current situation be assisting me to reach my north star? What's the silver lining? Change my mindset.

Re-Alignment
Am I on track? How can I realign or refocus to my north star?

Labelling Change
What stage of change am I currently experiencing?

My Current Priorities:
What are my current priorities? What's realistic for me to do right now?

Integration
Do these steps move me closer or further away from my north star?

Supporters:
My key supporters are:

PART 3 : CHANGING FOR SUCCESS

MY GOAL PLAN

Goal 1. Actions	By When	Who Involved
Milestone: I'll know I'm on track when:		

Goal 2. Actions	By When	Who Involved
Milestone: I'll know I'm on track when:		

Goal 3. Actions	By When	Who Involved
Milestone: I'll know I'm on track when:		

Goal 4. Actions	By When	Who Involved
Milestone: I'll know I'm on track when:		

Additional Actions/Notes:

What are you going to commit to doing tomorrow / this week in order to activate your action plan?

QUICKBITES INSIGHTS

The A4 process helps you to align your actions to your new knowledge – the key to successful change.

"Following the Breadcrumbs" means understanding the role of connectors to get you where you want to go.

Build the path from here to there through planning and goal setting.

Identify your supporters and key milestones. Take one step at a time and break the problem down into smaller parts to stop you from getting overwhelmed.

Goal setting is crucial to help you move towards your north star.

Use the QuickBites change and transition plan template to help you capture the key points and insights, and create your base line from which change can start.

PART 3 : CHANGING FOR SUCCESS

PERSONAL COMMITMENTS

To ensure you develop and build your skills in managing change, decide on some personal commitments now. What are you going to stop/start/continue in order to ensure your behaviour is aligned to your new level of knowledge?

Start	STOP	Continue

CHANGE - A Practical Guide

WRAP UP

What have been your key insights from this QuickBites book?

_____
_____
_____
_____
_____
_____
_____

What is the one thing you can do today to activate your learning?

_____
_____
_____
_____
_____
_____
_____

"Things do not change; we change."
-Henry David Thoreau

OTHER QUICKBITES TITLES

"Teams: A Practical Guide For Developing, Managing and Leading The High Performing Team."
By Robin Elliott

E Book, PDF and Print Book
https://quickbites.co/product-category/books/

Companion Product
Values Assessment Card Sort
https://quickbites.co/product-category/resources/

More titles coming on line soon.

WANT MORE INFORMATION?

Robin Elliott is available for keynote presentations and business coaching.

If you found this book useful the good news is we have more titles coming on line.

Register your details at www.quickbites.co for updates.

Contact info@quickbites.co

QUICKBITES
DIGESTIBLE BUSINESS LEARNING

www.ingramcontent.com/pod-product-compliance
Lightning Source LLC
Chambersburg PA
CBHW060015210526
45170CB00018B/3054